How to keep your wife

A little black book worth keeping

G.N. Thornton

Copyright © 2017 Black Stacks Publishing LLC

All rights reserved.

ISBN: 0-9989661-1-8

ISBN-13: 978-0-9989661-1-3

DEDICATION

This book is dedicated to my loving, brilliant and supportive husband Rich, the king of our castle, the love of my life. Thanks for being the wonderful man that you are. You love me unconditionally and as if that's not enough, you set a standard that no man could follow. You have exceeded all expectations of what a husband should be. All marriages go through rough patches and ours has not been exempt but, the way we handle our issues determines the outcome. I truly love and respect you for being that rock I could lean on that pillow I could rest on and the safe I could confide in. During the hard times, you make life much more palatable. I will forever love you unconditionally! Thank you, my love.

CONTENTS

Acknowledgments

1	Chapter Love your wife	1
2	Chapter Dinner guest	6
3	Chapter Be there for her	9
4	Chapter Compliment her	11
5	Chapter Surprise her	14
6	Chapter Understand her struggle	16
7	Chapter Communication	19
8	Chapter How to be heard	22
9	Chapter Togetherness	24
10	Chapter Room to grow	28

Preview of How to keep your Husband

ACKNOWLEDGMENTS

To God be the glory for all he has done for me in my life. I thank God even for the bad times, it was the bad times that made me think more ejectively. For the nights that I cried out your name and you answered, it wasn't what I wanted to hear yet you still answered. Thank you, Lord, for giving me guidance when others couldn't.

To my parents, William and Naomi Watts, you have been super supportive, loving and understanding. I love you both for the morals you have instilled in me. I grew-up watching your beautiful marriage as you raised us, kids, guiding us through our mishaps. We're grateful to have parents like you.

1 CHAPTER

First and foremost:

Number one:

Love your Wife:

The very first thing you need to decide is, do you want to keep your wife? If you need to, write down some pros and cons of keeping your wife. Once that's done if your pros outweigh your cons, you'll decide the marriage is worth salvaging. It's time to revitalize this relationship.

Guys, love your wife more than any sports or anyone else. I know you're thinking (of course I love her I married her, didn't I?) the fact that you married her just means you knew she had value and you didn't want her to marry someone else. You probably still love your wife but do you show it? Don't worry, this goes both ways I know. As women, we sometimes forget to tell you that we love you however we usually show it pretty well. Once you've been married for a few years, both men and women can become complacent. You made it, married have your kids a great career, everything is everything until it's not! You're not feeling the love, she pays more attention to the kids than she does you. She's changed, nothing seems the same. She keeps wearing that scarf that smells like hair spray to bed, never wears that sexy lingerie she used to wear.

Women are simpler than you think. When we act a certain way or stop doing something you like, you messed up! It might not be something that you did that day, most women have a high tolerance and tend to hold things inside. Here are just a few things that could be wrong:

][

1. Failed to give her a kiss or hug
2. Didn't speak when you walked in
3. Forgot her birthday
4. Forgot your anniversary
5. Didn't call or text all day
6. Didn't satisfy her sexual needs

If you do all six of the things listed above and still find yourself in trouble, you're not doing something right. Maybe, it's something you did in the past that she just hasn't gotten over. Did you cheat on her? Flirt in front of her? Neither of these is great ways to stay married, but they can be forgiven. I didn't say forgotten, women have strong memories when it comes to infidelity. If you cheated, confess. For some reason, women always find out, always! Women's intuition is amazing! If you flirt, stop! Your little feelings would be hurt if she did the same.

Maybe you did send your wife off right, with a hug and kiss or even a (have a great day honey), If this is done repetitively, it becomes redundant and if done emotionless you will need to switch things up. Wash the dishes after dinner, run her bath water, fix her a snack. It will surprise the heck out of her if she's the one who cooks all the time and she comes home and dinner is already done! Just because she may cook better than you, doesn't mean she wants to do it all the time. If she goes over to her girlfriend's house and her girl's hubby has prepared brunch for them, what do you think she expects. She's just praying that one day her husband would do something this special for her. Instead, when she has a guest you're upstairs calling down for her to bring you something to snack on. Just pitiful!

2 CHAPTER

Number two:

Dinner guest:

Please check with your wife before inviting people over for cooked meals, not because she might not want company, she needs to plan for her meals and make sure her house is clean, these are things that most men know nothing about. It's important to consult with your wife first trust me. The type of cleaning that she does just to get thru a work week, and the type of cleaning she does when expecting company are completely different. Her getting thru the week cleans are simple, clean the bathrooms wash the dishes sweep the floors do laundry. Expecting company: she cleans everything. Toilets, sweeps and mops the floor, dust the furniture, wipe down the walls, cabinets, ceiling fans, light fixtures, and doors. Why do you ask? Because if the house is dirty it doesn't matter that she just worked a 50-hour work week, she is still the one your guest will side eye if the house is not clean. Your friends and family members will talk behind her back and if they say something to you, shut that mess down ASAP! It is never ok for someone to talk smack about your wife no matter who they are. Just trust me on this one, give her some advance notice. If you invite someone to dinner a few hours before dinner, call your wife and let her know. A few hours' notice may be all she needs to have a cleaning crew stop by and make the house spotless. They won't clean the same way she does but at least they would have made the house appear to be clean. If you've ever used a cleaning service you know what I'm talking about.

3 CHAPTER

Number 3:

Be there for her:

Be available to talk to your wife always. Let's face it, women like to talk, sometimes you men just need to let us talk. Some of you all need to talk more. Honestly, let some emotions show! I don't mean crying like a blubbering fool all the time, but showing some kind of emotion is human, right?

If she calls in the middle of the day she might not want anything just misses you, accept her call. I end most of my calls to my husband with, "I didn't want anything".

I'm not telling you to break any rules at the job, if you can't talk on the phone that's fine she probably knows this, text her if at all possible. If you are online Facebooking or on Instagram, make a post for her, (a pic of the two of you), poke her. These gestures let her know her husband is thinking of her.

Also, if you read her post on a social media platform be the first to like or comment. You know you have her page on a notify alert coming straight to your phone. Women need confirmation every now and then, so just let us know you're thinking of us.

4 CHAPTER

Number four:

Compliment her:

Compliment your wife. Now understand, I'm not saying that every day you need to tell her she's the most beautiful woman in the world, no that's not what she wants, however; it won't hurt to tell her she looks great in that dress, or she looks nice. Women love to be complimented. If your wife gets dressed to go to work or just out with her girls. If you glance at her and think wow she looks real nice, trust me other men think she looks really nice too and guess what, they're going to tell her. You tell her before she leaves the house! Don't let another man tell your wife something that she doesn't hear from her own husband. I don't care what a woman says, we love compliments! Please make sure you are making your wife feel beautiful, even if she has on a pair of sweat pants and a headband. Tell her she's rocking those sweat pants. If you want to see her wear something different, why not pick up a pair of leggings or lounge wear of your choosing. Now let's be clear, I don't care what Beyoncé said, we are not going to be cooking your dinner in our high-heels. Well, we might do it on some occasions but don't think we're going to keep doing it. We love you but, no.

Why are women expected to stay glammed up while the man puts on anything they want? Our hair, outfits, make-up, and attitudes must always be on point. We need some dress down days too!

5 CHAPTER

Number five:

Surprise her:

Surprise her, it doesn't have to be a huge surprise like a party. Buy Her flowers send them to her job or bring them home. Get her a gift basket or something. Take her out on the town, and be sure to hold her/hug her while out. Public display of affection is wonderful! Women are not really complicated; some men just need to up their game. I know you've heard it before, but here it goes again. Do all the things you did when you were trying to get her. Don't wonder why she's switched up if you stop treating her the way she was used to being treated. This doesn't mean buying her stuff and things, but if you used to buy her flowers every week and now she can't even get a rose on her birthday, you need to check yourself! Women like nice things but you are not required to give them to us on a regular basis. Most women will agree, it's the small stuff that counts the most. Run her bath water, rub her feet, wash her hair, polish her toes. All that's good stuff. If you don't want to do any of these, hey the next best thing is to have someone else do it. Send her to the spa for some down time. It will be much appreciated and once she's revitalized she will be ready to return to the demanding world of marriage.

6 CHAPTER

Number six:

Understand her struggle:

This chapter is for the married with children couples:

It is hard enough being a woman, then we get pregnant and become superwoman! We cook, clean, socialize, work full-time jobs then come home and cater to your ego, and your sexual desires. No, maybe we're not superwoman, we're wonder woman, wondering how in the world we accomplish so much without falling dead!

How to Keep your Wife

Be grateful men, most of you couldn't make it a day in our shoes even if we are stay-at-home moms no, especially if we are stay-at-home moms. You might think all we do is sit on the sofa watching reality tv or something. We actually don't have a lot of time for that, between washing and folding clothes, cleaning the house and fixing dinner. We still may have to pick up the kids from school, feed them a snack, take them to whatever after school activity you signed them up for, knowing you would seldom be the one to take them. Hey, you know that old saying "It takes a village to raise a kid"? Well, if it takes a village how do you expect the woman to raise them on their own? Give us a little help please sir. We really have no desire to raise our children alone, it's not enough for you to tell them to listen to their mother. It's good that you tell them to listen to us, but we need you to also be there for them not just for the discipline, but also to show them loyalty, and love. If you don't know by now, kids don't want to listen to what you say, you have to show them! Don't tell them to respect their mother if you're not respecting their mother. That two-way street will backfire on you. Show respect to your child's mother even if she's not a good mother. If the two of you are not together unless your child is 18yrs of age or older, chances are you will have to communicate with this woman, and you don't want your kid/children to see you acting a fool and disrespecting her.

7 CHAPTER

Number seven:

Communication:

The key to a happy, healthy relationship is communication, and the key to communication is learning how to talk to people. If you are a poor communicator you may struggle in your relationship or your wife will 1. Completely run the relationship or 2. Feel totally alienated. While you don't want one person to completely run the relationship, you also don't want anyone to feel alienated while in the relationship.

Feeling alienated may lead your spouse to talk to other people about how she's feeling, you don't want this to happen. Never, ever put an outsider in your relationship!

If you aren't going to marriage counseling, there is no reason to speak with anyone other than your spouse about your spouse, especially if the topic is one of a sensitive nature like intimacy. If you decide to break this relationship rule, please don't talk to the one friend or family member who knows everyone's business and blabs it all at the family reunion! This will wreak havoc on your relationship, and cause your spouse not to trust you. My mother once told me, "never tell anyone anything about your spouse that you wouldn't want that person repeating". I've taken heed to her advice. Here's one thing I know, people judge others for something they believe to be true even if it's not. So, don't assume that something is the truth when in doubt ask questions. Don't be accusatory.

8 CHAPTER

Number eight:

How to be heard:

Talking loud or speaking rudely to your spouse does not mean you are being heard, it means you are acting like a jack-ass. This will only cause an argument and as we all know, she will win. This doesn't help the relationship, do this instead: Take your wife's hands lead her to a seat or even better, you take a seat on the sofa and have her sit on your lap. This move will get her guard down, that's where you want it. Talk to her calmly, ask her what's going on with her. She will be more likely to politely let you know how she's feeling, at the same time you can voice all your issues in a loving way.

Remember, if your needs aren't being met, chances are somewhere along the way you messed up! In no way do I think men should be able to read their wives mind, however; you should be able to read body language. You know your spouse better than anyone, so why wouldn't you know if she's unhappy. She knows when somethings off with you even if she doesn't say anything. Your wife will go out of her way to make you happy, you need to do the same.

9 CHAPTER

Number 9:

Togetherness:

To keep the spice in your life be sure to include date night. I can remember when my husband and I used to let our date nights turn into family night. I know that's crazy but my baby girl always wanted to bust in on our night and once she's in the room all the other kids follow and we end up watching a family movie. We had to learn that date night is not a night to hang out with the children, it's a night to hang with each other and enjoy one another's company. Put on your best attitude get dressed up if you'd like and take your wife out on the town. We learned that for date night, we needed to leave the comforts of our home and actually do something. If your wife is spontaneous, try packing her bag for a quick getaway. If you know she has nightly rituals that can't be broken don't forget to pack what she needs, facial cream, makeup bag etc... don't worry if you forget some toiletries they can easily be picked up along the way. If you're planning a weekend getaway out of the country or maybe just to the Caribbean, don't forget her passport and her favorite carry-on bag. If she takes medication, better bring that too. By the time you get to the airport or the port, she'll know somethings up, have her check her purse for anything that might cause a security concern. She'll probably be looking around wondering if you packed her things. Trust me, she'll be surprised and will more than likely be curious about this impromptu trip. If she gets upset because you've somehow derailed her weekend, you might want to be asking some questions of your own. Unless you're a total jerk, what woman would give their husband attitude about planning a getaway? Maybe a cheating wife would if she'd planned to get away that weekend, but that's another book for some other time. The grateful wife would love for her husband to plan anything, a trip to the mall or the other side of town would do if you're planning it for her. My point is oftentimes women are left to plan everything from dinner to family vacation, to a trip to the dentist, so if our husbands take time to say, hey honey, I thought it would be nice if I could take you on a cruise would that be ok with you? Of course, and yes!! should be the only answers you hear. After that a stream of questions like When are we leaving and for how long, have you already booked, what should I bring?

Guys, she will take it from here, find a baby sitter, pack for the both of you and even find all the hotspots at your destination.

For clues on places or things your wife might enjoy, listen to what she talks about. Ask her during small talk one night, she doesn't have to know that you're taking note of said places. Be smart and be considerate.

10 CHAPTER

Number Ten:

Room to grow:

Just because you're married doesn't give you the right to relax. Women don't get to relax, even after we give birth, we might fall off the upkeep wagon for a little while especially if we are forced to be down longer due to birthing complications, but most of us are in the birthing room trying to fix our hair or face. We're constantly trying to come up with new ways to keep our appearance in tip top conditions. I say all that to say this, we all have room for improvement! No one is perfect. If you're being honest with yourself you know you're not perfect, some of you may be wondering how you managed to snag such a fabulous wife? She might be wondering how she managed to snag such a fabulous husband. Trust and believe that most of the thoughts that cross your mind also have crossed hers at some point.

Remember, you're in a relationship, stay positive and chase her as hard as you chased her when you first started dating. If she stopped doing some of those things you loved so much, trust me she will do them again but you must stay active. Show all the love and affection that you wish to receive. Stay motivated.

This book was intended to help you stay happily married for years to come. Don't be afraid to jump right in and fall in love with your spouse over and over again.

The End.

Thanks for reading! If I was able to help anyone, I hope it was you!

Let me know what you think about this book if you liked it hated it or would like me to address a specific topic.

Email me at www.books@gnthornton.com

Bonus Preview:

How to keep your Husband

10 Steps to a happy home

Chapter 1

To keep or not to keep:

The question of all questions is, do you want to keep your husband? How do you know if you want to keep your husband?

1. He completes you
2. You can't imagine life without him
3. You love him
4. His good qualities out way the bad habits

For a better evaluation of how you feel about your husband try spending a few days away from him if possible, don't just abandon him. When you return home, make your decision to stay or to go.

Whatever the reason, if your answer is yes you want to keep your husband you need to prepare yourself to work for your marriage.

If you take your vows seriously, you would try to work out any issues you may have with your husband. The fact is this, people today are quick to divorce. Marriage should not be disposable! if you take some time to understand the actions being taken, you'll come to realize that divorce is avoidable.

What is the one thing that women everywhere say they can't get past in a relationship?

Infidelity! He cheated, but is he a cheater or did he cheat? What's the difference? If he's a master manipulator he is most likely a cheater. Be careful when trying to judge a book by its cover you'd be surprised at who the cheaters actually are. Did he find himself in a situation and come to tell you about it. Let's just be real, no he is not going to tell you about it even if it just happened once. Even if he's a very honest man, he won't mumble a word unless you ask. Sometimes we get too comfortable in our relationships so without even thinking about it we put our man on the back burner. Not to say you forget about him completely, but you just kind of go on about your life, working and taking care of the kids, running the household. This leaves your husband disengaged. Understand there is no excuse for cheating and I do not condone it I'm not trying to encourage anyone to condone a cheater, I simply want to point out that there is no perfect man or woman for that matter, but there can be a near perfect marriage. I did say near perfect. This is not some fairytale ladies and we do need to own up to the major role we play as wives. So many women think that marriage is about the wedding and reception, but marriage is actually about what goes on after the wedding, not the honeymoon I mean the life after. The marriage is the give and take, the hustle and bustle, the wrong and the right. You can't just walk away from marriage, you need to stay and fight.

Infidelity is a big one, pair that with a baby ooooh, now that's drama! But let me tell you something a wise woman once said, "there are many women who have stayed with their husbands after infidelity. That they stayed doesn't mean they are weak. They were not the first to be cheated on, and they won't be the last." It doesn't have to break you, it can make you and your marriage much stronger. Love is not enough for marriage if that's all you have is the way you feel about someone I'm sorry to tell you this, but feelings can fade away with time. You will need to develop a connection so real that even when your man has gotten on your last nerve you can still say, I'm here for you honey.

ABOUT THE AUTHOR

G.N. Thornton was born Grace Naomi Watts in, Washington N.C. raised in Indianapolis, In.

I'm a married mother of 6 wonderful children. I have 3 biological children and 3 step-children. I don't like the label (step-children) so in most cases I refrain from using it.

I write both fiction and non-fiction. I like fairy tales and romance. I love to give advice especially if it's something I know a lot about like children, relationships, and marriage. I've been married for 10 years. I was raised by two very loving parents who have been married for 47 years. I believe in the power of marriage, if done right it gives your life perfect peace. I love to see people happily married.

www.ingramcontent.com/pod-product-compliance
Lightning Source LLC
Chambersburg PA
CBHW022347040426
42449CB00006B/756